Innovation in Agriculture
Social Media Techniques

Table of Contents

The first rule of any technology used in a business is that automation applied to an efficient operation will magnify the efficiency. The second is that automation applied to an inefficient operation will magnify the inefficiency.

— Bill Gates

Chapter 1. Introduction

In an era where technology intertwines with every corner of our lives, even the agricultural industry, rooted deeply in traditional practices, has not been left untouched. Welcome to our captivating special report on "Innovation in Agriculture: Social Media Techniques." This comprehensive piece delves into the refreshing integration of modern social media techniques reshaping the pastoral landscapes around us. Brimming with case studies, expert insights, and clear guidelines, it brings to you an inspiring blend of the old and the new. This special report embodies a unique journey worth embarking on, no matter whether you're a tech-savvy farmer, an agribusiness professional, or simply an enthusiast interested in learning about the dynamic shifts stirring the earth under our feet. And trust us, by the end of it, you won't just be educated, you'll be motivated to contribute to this digital revolution in agriculture yourself! So why wait? Step into the future of farming today, one hashtag at a time.

Chapter 2. The Rising Digital Trends in Agriculture

Our world has been ceaselessly endeavoring towards accomplishing more profound technological prosperity. True to this trend, the agricultural industry, forming the nurturant backbone of our society, has been graced by the advent of various digital trends, all promising to add a touch of innovation to the traditional practices that have survived for millennia.

2.1. The Intersection of Agriculture and Technology

Agricultural practices have evolved dramatically throughout history, from stone-age hoe farming to the modern crop-breeding techniques. Ancient civilizations saw the inception of farm domestication, irrigation methods, and the use of beasts for plowing. The era of industrial revolution brought about mechanization to the field, while the late 20th century witnessed the green revolution, characterized by the application of genetics in enhancing crop yield.

The dawn of the 21st century, however, is experiencing an unprecedented crossroad - a fusion of agriculture and technology, termed as a major facet of Industry 4.0. The term ''Agritech'' has gained ubiquitous recognition, converging farming methods with breakthroughs in digital technology. 'Agritech' encapsulates a multitude of advancements, including precision farming, Internet of Things (IoT) devices, big data analytics, and the use of Artificial Intelligence and Drones in farming, to name a few.

2.2. Embracing Digital Platforms: Social Media in Agriculture

One of the most significant elements of the digital era is social media, the use of which transcends borders and industries – agriculture being no exception. Today, farmers, merchants, researchers, enthusiasts, and consumers alike have recognized its potential for fostering a digital agricultural community. Virtual markets have transformed the traditional roadside blueprint, and platforms like Facebook Marketplace and eBay allow the direct marketing of local produce. Twitter harvests trending conversations and hashtags around farming, helping propagate agricultural news and policies on a global scale.

Agricultural extension services have found a reliable ally in YouTube, which demonstrates everything from tool utilization to crop maintenance techniques via accessible videos. WhatsApp groups allow real-time intra and inter-farm communication for speedy decisions, while still offering a window to the larger agricultural world. And let's not forget Instagram, allowing farmers to delineate their journey - photos of ripening crops, videos of dairy procedures, or stories of harvest festivals can be shared, reaching diverse groups around the world at the click of a button.

2.3. The Many Faces of Mobile Apps in Agriculture

Mobile applications deserve a special mention in our exploration of the agricultural digital landscape. They've tapped into several layers of the industry, and their capabilities are still expanding. While some apps offer advice on pest management or yield forecasting, others educate on cattle nutrition. There are platforms to sell used agricultural machinery or buy raw manure. Functions like tracking weather patterns or monitoring soil quality have provided a massive boost to precision farming. The advent of mobile applications has indeed contributed to a tremendous increase in overall farm productivity.

2.4. Unleashing the Power of Big Data in Agriculture

Agriculture is now entering the era of big data. With technologies like IoT making headway in farming practices, data accumulation from numerous sources has been made possible. Insights derived from this information have begun to positively affect farming at both, micro and macro levels.

The data, when analyzed effectively, can contribute to better understanding crop patterns and predicting yields, thus helping farmers make informed decisions about their planting and harvesting schedules. It also provides significant inputs for governments and organizations, helping them devise appropriate agricultural policies and strategies.

2.5. Shaping the Future: Artificial Intelligence and Drones

Artificial Intelligence (AI) and drones might still be relatively new entrants into the agricultural field, but they're making substantial contributions. AI is being employed for various applications, from crop and soil monitoring to predictive analytics. Robots and machine learning algorithms are being used for weed control and precision farming.

Drones have become an economical and efficient method of surveying farms and providing real-time data for better decision-making. Other benefits include soil erosion tracking or plant health monitoring, dramatically easing the burden of manual work.

In conclusion, the digital trends in agriculture are indeed a testament to our evolving civilization. They've truly revolutionized the agricultural landscape, steering it towards sustainability, efficiency, and global connectedness. Technology assumes the mantle of a powerful aid, promising to mitigate the challenges faced by the agricultural sector and paving the way for a prosperous and secure food future. Each digital trend carries a unique potential, waiting only to be appropriately harnessed, helping us reimagine the infinite possibilities of the agricultural realm in the years to come.

Chapter 3. Understanding Social Media: A Primer

In today's hyperconnected world, where information is propagated at unprecedented speeds, understanding the crux of social media dynamics has become not just relevant, but crucial. This is more true when it comes to sectors such as agriculture, where rapid advancements have revolutionized traditional practices. As we embark on the journey of demystifying social media, one must first appreciate its technological roots, myriad platforms, the nature of its powerful reach, and its social ramifications.

3.1. Technological Roots of Social Media

In the garage of a suburban house, in 1971, the first-ever email was sent from one computer to another, marking the dawn of digital communication. From that point onward, technology began a ceaseless march towards more sophisticated modes of interaction. From internet relay chats (IRCs) in the 1980s to the rise of discussion forums and blogs in the 1990s, the groundwork was gradually laid for the birth of today's social media.

Fast forward to the early 2000s, a series of revolutionary platforms sprung onto the scene. Facebook, Twitter, and YouTube, among others, redefined communication at a global scale. These platforms enabled the seamless exchange of text, images, and videos, thereby making social media the go-to platform for personalized and diverse communication.

Next came the exponential proliferation of smartphones, causing an astronomical surge in social media usage. Coupled with the advancement in internet technologies, such as the transition from 3G to 4G and now on the cusp of 5G, the world became a global village thanks to social media's ubiquitous reach.

3.2. The Multiplicity and Utility of Platforms

Part of the appeal of social media lies in its multiplicity of platforms, each offering distinct tools and garnering unique demographics. From Facebook's versatile timeline and user-friendly interface that captivates all age groups to Instagram's visually-driven feed attracting the artistically inclined younger generation, from strategic networking via LinkedIn to the breakneck-paced Twitter sparking real-time debates — all these platforms serve a myriad of needs.

Then there's YouTube, TikTok, Snapchat, each offering riveting media consumption experiences; Reddit delivering discussions with deep dives into niche topics; Pinterest igniting creativity with its well-organized ideation boards. Not forgetting WhatsApp, WeChat, and Messenger, which allow intimate and immediate personal and group communication.

3.3. The Mighty Reach of Social Media

Social media's influence can be measured in numbers and reach. As of 2021, there are over 3.8 billion social media users worldwide, accounting for nearly half the global population. These platforms transcend borders, cultures, languages, and time zones, therefore presenting an irresistible playground for influence and engagement.

Through social media, conversations spark spontaneously at any instant around any topic. Virality, a wonder child of the internet age, works its magic in propagating information or misinformation within the blink of an eye, commanding the attention of millions.

3.4. Social Ramifications of Social Media

The impacts of social media go far beyond communication and transcend into tangible societal developments. Over time, social media has democratized information dissemination, creating increased transparency and giving a voice to the voiceless, thereby imposing checks and balance on institutions. It has also given rise to influencer culture, transforming marketing on its head, pushing businesses to adopt more personable, authentic, and interactive outreach strategies.

At the same time, the perils of social media are equally palpable. From fake news, cyberbullying, privacy invasion, to addictive usage and mental health implications, the dark side of social media is a stark reminder that every technology, while a tool for progress, poses potential threats to societal well-being if left unchecked.

This comprehensive exploration of social media's origins, its diverse platforms, extensive reach, and societal implications, positions you better to appreciate the potential impact it can have when leveraged judiciously in the field of agriculture. As we progress in subsequent chapters, we will fine-tune our spotlight on specifics of how these platforms are being harnessed to revolutionize the agricultural world.

Next up, "Influencing Agriculture Through Social Media: An Overview" offers a captivating look at how farmers, agriculturists and the entire agribusiness industry can optimize social media use to enhance their activities, impact, and profitability. Buckle up for an enlightening journey into an innovative and technologically-driven agricultural landscape — all via the medium of social media.

Chapter 4. Influencing Agriculture Through Social Media: An Overview

The dawn of the digital age has rendered traditional boundaries almost non-existent. Even the most labor-intensive practices like agriculture are being influenced, and quite significantly so, by the surge of the digital world, a world that seems expansive yet conveniently accessible because of the magic of social media. In this chapter, we will undertake an exhausting exploration into the influence of social media on agriculture and give a detailed overview of the matter.

4.1. Understanding the Scope of Influence

Social media isn't a trend anymore; it's a fact of life. Its charm has even managed to bedazzle traditional farming practices. Whether it's Facebook, Twitter, Instagram, LinkedIn, or YouTube, all these platforms are being increasingly utilized by farmers, agribusinesses, stakeholders, and everyone in between to boost the agricultural sector. The scope of influence encompasses various aspects such as planning, decision-making, marketing, continuous learning, advocacy, and fostering a sense of community among the agricultural population.

4.2. A Farmer's Best Digital Friend

In traditional times, a farmer's best friend could have been their livestock or their most productive piece of land. In the age of digital farming, it's increasingly becoming their smartphone. Personal experiences, farming innovations, weather forecasting, market updates, all are shared on social media platforms, providing a toolbox of information on a global scale. From advices on the right seeds to plant for a particular season to discussions around new sustainable farming technologies, it acts as a ubiquitous knowledge repository, coming to the aid of farmers around the globe.

4.3. Farmers as Content Creators and Consumers

Notably, the farmers aren't just consumers of digital information. They have also embraced their roles as content creators by sharing their daily farming activities, successful experiments, and novel farming techniques which are sometimes couched in humor and wit, making them more accessible to a wider audience.

4.4. The Power of Hashtags

When a popular social media influencer uses a hashtag, it can stir a wave of influence impacting millions of followers. The same principle applies to the agricultural sector. Hashtags like #AgTech, #CropScience, #FarmLife, etc., have substantial reach and frequency and serve as virtual venues for conversation and knowledge exchange about best practices, novel technologies, and challenges faced by the community.

4.5. Social Media as a Marketing Tool

Social media not only provides a knowledge platform but also a vibrant marketplace. From selling fresh farm produce on Facebook to farmers engaging with potential customers on Instagram, it allows farmers to bypass middlemen and market their produce directly, thus ensuring better profits and fostering an emotional connection with the consumer.

4.6. Advocacy and Awareness

The role of social media extends beyond the farm gate. As the world tackles various challenges related to food security, climate change, and sustainable farming practices, social media allows for the stimulation of conversations, garnering support for causes, spreading awareness, and influencing policy change. It empowers ordinary people to voice their concerns, thereby promoting activism at a grassroots level.

4.7. Strengthening the Agri-Community

Perhaps one of the key influences of social media on agriculture has been the cultivation of a strong, interactive, and supportive agricultural community. Knowledge exchange forums, support groups, online farm tours, webinars – they all foster a sense of unity, provide moral support, and uplift community spirit, acting as a digital agri-cooperative.

As we conclude this detailed examination of the stimulating influence social media holds over agriculture, it is undeniable that the digital landscape has redrawn the boundaries of traditional farming practices. Its potential to foster innovation, spread knowledge, influence policies and cultivate a sense of community is unparalleled. However, it also presents unique challenges that require astute digital engagement strategies, which will be the focus of our next section.

Chapter 5. Effective Social Media Techniques in Modern Farming

As we initiate this all-embracing discourse, it is pertinent to understand that the seismic shift towards digitization has dramatically altered the way we pursue and perceive agriculture. The vanguard of this change is social media, the sword-arm of modern communication. We will be dissecting this broad umbrella into functional fragments, aiming at shedding light into the effective social media techniques deployed in the realm of modern farming. Let's embark on this enlightening exploration – buckle-up for a meticulous journey through the symphony of 280 characters, emoji reactions, virality, trends, blue ticks, and hashtags that are revolutionizing crop fields worldwide.

5.1. The Power of Connectivity

Through social media, the world has been made smaller – turning into a global village where everyone can interact with anyone, no matter the distance or divide. For farmers, the roots of connectivity have penetrated deep into the soil of their fields. From exchanging information about crop prices on Twitter, showcasing new farming techniques on Instagram, to conducting live Q&A sessions about sustainable farming on Facebook, the platforms for connectivity are endless and are being harnessed in innovative manners to sow the seeds of information, germinate ideas, grow businesses, and cultivate communities.

5.2. Knowledge Sharing and Expert Advice

Sub-platforms such as Facebook Groups, LinkedIn Professional Groups, or Twitter threads have evolved as the contemporary seminar halls where experts share their views, address queries, provide recommendations, and engage in informed dialogues in real-time. Farmers can join groups specific to their crops, regions, or interests and profit from the wealth of knowledge shared by the community. This has turned social media from a passive broadcast medium into an active engagement hub where content is not just consumed but also created, critiqued, and collaborated upon.

5.3. Marketing, Networking, and Advocacy

In the market sector bustling with competition, farmers, agripreneurs, and agritech companies have been using social media to amplify their voices, advertise their products, attract investments, network with contemporaries, lobby with policymakers, and advocate for their rights. By giving businesses personified voices, social platforms have added a new dimension to marketing, reputation management, and brand building, making the interaction more relatable, emotional, and lucrative.

5.4. Showcasing the Process

Content such as 'From Seed to Table' or 'Behind The Scenes' videos posted on YouTube, TikTok, or Instagram have been making viewers part of the journey rather than end consumers. They offer transparency and build trust about the product while educating the viewers about farming. By narrating the story behind the produce, these videos add an element of empathy to the consumption, culminating in increased consumer loyalty and product empathy.

5.5. Online Selling

E-commerce has entered farm fields too. Social media platforms like Facebook and Instagram now facilitate direct online selling through 'Social Shops.' This eliminates intermediaries, offering a better return on produce for farmers while consumers benefit from fresh produce straight from the farm. Also, it provides a platform for farmers to sell their products globally, thereby enlarging their customer base significantly.

5.6. Crowd Sourcing and Crowd Funding

Farmers are increasingly tapping into the powers of the crowd. Be it for solving problems collectively, garnering support for a cause, or funding an initiative through platforms like GoFundMe, social media lets farmers seek assistance and provide support in an unprecedented manner.

5.7. AI and Big Data

As AI and big data start permeating farming, social media platforms offer an expanse of data to be mined for agricultural understanding, prediction, management, and improvement. Crucially, these platforms provide a crucial solution for data sourcing as well as effective channels for implementing findings and solutions.

But with the plethora of opportunities also comes challenges, the digital divide, privacy concerns, misinformation, and the risk of cyber threats. As modern farming walks the social media path, it needs to tread along carefully, with cognizance of its potential pitfalls. Social media, as a tool, holds immense promise to revolutionize agriculture, but its prudent harnessing will shape the course it takes.

Clearly, the realm of social media is as vast as it is varied. However, armed with the right tools, knowledge, and strategies, it can be an incredibly effective way to enhance agricultural practices, increase yield, and influence change. Thus, march on, reader, for the future of farming is but a 'soft touch' swipe away.

Chapter 6. Case Studies: Successful Utilization of Social Media in Agriculture

The past decade has witnessed an unprecedented surge in the adoption of social media as an engagement tool in the realm of agriculture. Whether employed to disseminate information, foster innovation, encourage collaboration, or rally advocacy, this online landscape of hashtags and handles has transformed how those who plow the earth connect, function, and thrive. This chapter presents an array of compelling case studies detailing how different agricultural entities, varying from individual farmers to international agribusinesses, have pulled off successful utilization of social media to sprout change and show the world the potential lying within our age-old soils through new age wires.

6.1. Embracing Innovation and Community Spirit: The Story of Farmer Fred

Farmer Fred's story is emblematic of individual farmers harnessing the power of social media for agricultural success. Joining Twitter under the handle @FarmerFred, he began sharing striking images from his daily farm life. But these were just the seeds he sowed. The genuine understanding and appreciation of his work came to fruition when he implemented modern farming techniques. As viewers remained glued to the dramatic transformation of his once traditional farm, Fred gained followers rapidly, becoming a credible influencer whose techniques were replicated far and wide.

6.2. AgriMega: An Agribusiness Giant Tapping into the Power of Social Media

Directly contrasting Farmer Fred, we have AgriMega, an established behemoth in the agricultural industry, choosing a different route. Realizing the need to build a more personal and community-based rapport with their online followers, they started their #MyAgriJourney campaign on Instagram. Encouraging farmers to share their agricultural narratives, the hashtags soon trended, creating an empathetic connect between the brand and the producers, consumers alike, and painting AgriMega as a caring corporate citizen.

6.3. Farming Facts: A Social Media Advocate Enlightening the Deluded

Moving away from personal tales and corporate narratives, the focus now shifts to Farming Facts, a Facebook page that produces easily digestible visual content clarifying misconceptions surrounding the agricultural industry. The page, which now has more than a million followers, has not only helped in debunking myths about farming practices, but has also increased the general public's understanding of, and respect for, agriculture and food production.

6.4. The Power of YouTube: The Agri-Edutainment Channel

The Agri-Edutainment YouTube channel stands as the embodiment of inventive learning through social engagement. It presents a plethora of content ranges from how-to videos, virtual farm tours, interviews with agricultural experts to live Q&A sessions. The interactive functionality of YouTube coupled with engaging and educative video content turned the channel into a virtual classroom, bringing the marvels and mysteries of farming to millions of screens across the planet.

6.5. LinkedIn Agriculture Community: A Creditworthy Network

Our final case study hones in on the professional social media platform LinkedIn and its large, amenable network of agricultural enthusiasts, professionals, scholars, and business owners. Participating in discussions, finding career opportunities, engaging with sector developments, and even securing agri-oriented funding, this platform brings out the practical, tangible benefits of connecting on social media.

In conclusion, social media's role in reshaping the agricultural landscape has been nothing short of revolutionary. These case studies present a glimpse of the significant potential and positive impact social media has had within this realm. They collectively signal towards the imperative future where every stakeholder in the agricultural field should consider the 'field' of social media as integral to their growth and success as the very fields they till. After all, in the modern era, farming isn't just about the soil and seed, it's about tweets and feeds.

Chapter 7. The Role of Influencers and Bloggers in Agricultural Promotion

In the ever-evolving landscape of agricultural promotion, the role of influencers and bloggers has grown exponentially. The rise of social media platforms has enabled a fresh perspective on how we perceive, interact with, and learn about agriculture. Acquiring the services of a blogger, vlogger, or social media influencer has now become an effective means of disseminating information, influencing perspectives, and shaping farming methods—spreading from the traditional grid of a local community to a global level.

7.1. The Power of Influence

It's easy to underestimate the power that influencers wield, but the ability to shape opinion and dictate trends should not be taken lightly. These are individuals who have built up a reputation in their chosen field and have subsequently amassed a following of individuals who trust and rely on their judgment. They can influence their followers by sharing their personal experiences and opinions on various subjects, agriculture being no exception.

Influencers can be anyone from famous celebrities endorsing eco-friendly agricultural products to an experienced farmer offering savvy tips about organic farming on a YouTube channel. What's paramount about influencers resides in their authenticity and the trust they've built with their follower-base, allowing their messages to resonate with the audience more profoundly than traditional advertising.

7.2. Bloggers: Fostering Bi-directional Communication

Bloggers, on the other hand, offer a slightly different, but equally potent, media channel. Where influencers juggle between inspirational contents, tutorials, product reviews, and more, bloggers tend to stick to informative, engaging articles with a higher focus on providing in-depth knowledge.

Blogs about agriculture can cover a wide range of topics extending from farming practices, environmental impacts, to policy discussions. They allow for more detailed communication about complex processes and concepts that may not be touched on traditional media. Blogs breed interaction by encouraging readers to comment, forming a community of engaged audience capable of valuable discourse, feedback, and even collaboration on agricultural matters.

7.3. Case Examples of Agricultural Influence through Social Media

An excellent example of agricultural influence is Zach Johnson, the 'Millennial Farmer'. Johnson is a fifth generation family farmer from Minnesota who's gained popularity on YouTube for sharing day-to-day farming operations and challenges, market trends, agricultural technologies and advocating for farming awareness and appreciation— planting a connection between the agricultural process and the reader in a way that mass media simply cannot.

Another example is 'Farm Babe', also known as Michelle Miller, who uses Facebook, Twitter, and her blog to debunk myths about modern farming practices and promote agricultural sciences. She works to bridge the gap between farmers and consumers, and has thus far been successful in her mission: cultivating an understanding of the farming issues amongst her audience that wouldn't have been possible without the power of social media.

7.4. The Benefits of Collaborating with Influencers and Bloggers

When agricultural organizations collaborate with influencers and bloggers, they're not just getting an endorsement, but are harnessing a community of trust. These collaborations can help tailor the message to bolster the values of sustainable farming, demystify the process of agricultural production and promote new, innovative technologies in agriculture for a wider audience.

Furthermore, influencers and bloggers can also bring to light the narratives of farmers—a sector of the community that has been previously marginalized from mainstream media. Their stories of struggle and resilience, triumph, and innovation, can educate the public about the realities of farming, igniting empathy and appreciation for the industry.

7.5. Challenges of Influencer Marketing in Agriculture

Whilst it is essential to harness the power of influencers and bloggers in agriculture, it's equally crucial to bear in mind the challenges these collaborations might yield. Authenticity, credibility, and accuracy of disseminated information become a concern. Miscommunication or misrepresentation of agricultural concepts can result in public mistrust discrediting not just the influencer, but also the collaborating agricultural body.

Additionally, the fluctuating nature of social media preference poses another challenge. Changes in platform's algorithm, loss of audience interest, and shifts in consumer behavior can all potentially affect the influencer's reach and effectiveness.

7.6. Conclusions and Future Prospects

Despite potential pitfalls, the collaboration between agriculture and social media influencers and bloggers seems a fruitful one. Nurturing such relationships could facilitate creating an environment where every influencer acts responsibly and provides properly sourced, accurate information, thereby fostering a culture of informed dialogue about agriculture.

In the future, we could envisage even more potent partnerships between farmers, influencers, and researchers to continue transforming the narrative surrounding agriculture, making it more accessible, relatable, and transparent. Thus, by harnessing the combined powers of digital and agrarian sectors, we can bring farther-forward our vision for a prosperous, sustainable, and informed agricultural landscape.

Chapter 8. Social Media for Agricultural Advocacy and Education

A strong grasp of contemporary technology is increasingly pivotal in today's dynamic agricultural landscape. And, just as they've transformed myriad sectors globally, social media platforms now shed light on ways we can advocate and educate about agriculture in novel, exciting ways.

8.1. Advocacy through Social Media

With the advent of the digital age, we are living in increasingly interconnected societies. This connectivity extends to agricultural communities as well, with farmers, agribusiness professionals, policy-makers and hobbyist gardeners all being part of the conversation. The ability to connect, express and persuade is now just a click away, creating unprecedented opportunities for advocacy.

The use of social media for advancing agricultural causes has been on the rise. Facebook, Twitter, Instagram, LinkedIn and other such platforms provide fertile ground where seeds of ideas can be sown and grown. They provide arenas for sharing success stories, promoting sustainable practices, and emphasizing the role of agriculture in food security and the economy.

Common social media tools for advocacy include creating and participating in discussions (via posts, tweets, and comments), using hashtags to extend reach, and developing viral campaigns around agricultural causes. For instance, a movement advocating organic production could leverage Facebook to raise awareness, create groups and events, and disseminate informational materials. Twitter, with its succinct format, can help promote causes by making them trend, while Instagram, with its visual focus, can serve to showcase healthy harvests and innovative farming techniques.

8.2. Agricultural Education and Social Media

In the realm of education, social media can serve as a potent vehicle for transmitting knowledge. In the context of agriculture, this can be executed by spreading information on new farming techniques, crop health, sustainable practices, and more. Here, every like, retweet, or share amounts to exponential learning.

YouTube, for example, has proven to be a formidable resource for agricultural education. In-depth tutorials on farming techniques, replanting, crop rotation, and the like, are readily available for anyone who seeks them. Likewise, blogs and podcasts provide an extensive array of comprehensive agricultural edification, sharing expert insights, interviews, emerging trends, and research in a friendly, accessible manner.

Each of these platforms has its strengths — YouTube excels in delivering visual content, podcasts offer mobile-friendly listening experiences, blogs provide a platform for long-form content, while Twitter, Facebook, and Instagram are perfect for bite-sized, shareable nuggets of information.

Online forums and discussion platforms (Reddit being a popular example) provide opportunities to initiate and take part in subject-focused conversations. Farmers can exchange practical tips, share their experiences, or crowdsource solutions to challenges they face in their local conditions.

8.3. Utilizing Social Media Platforms for Engagement

Utilization of social media in the agricultural sector isn't simply about being online. It's about engagement, which is a critical aspect of both advocacy and education.

Engagement measures whether people are receiving, interacting with, and being swayed by the content. It generally involves creating relevant content, ensuring active participation and nurturing constructive dialogue.

Farmers and agribusinesses can employ robust content strategies, which may include regular posts or videos on farming innovations, organic/sustainable practices and so on. Key metrics such as "likes," "shares," "comments," and "views" help gauge the levels of engagement, providing valuable insights to enhance outreach.

It's crucial to cultivate not just followers, but active participants. Many successful agricultural accounts use weekly hashtags such as #FarmFactFriday or #SustainableSunday to stimulate user interaction. Frequent responses to comments or messages, hosting occasional live Q&A sessions, or submitting guest posts can foster a sense of community, turning mere followers into ardent brand advocates.

Most importantly, the essence of social media advocacy and education in agriculture is openness to two-way communication. In other words, learning is reciprocal. Social media users have a wealth of firsthand, local, and experiential knowledge to share in return, enriching the learning ecosystem, fostering innovation, and bridging gaps between tradition and modernity in agriculture.

8.4. Conclusion

In the age of technology, the agricultural landscape continues to evolve, and the integration of social media into these traditional practices signifies an exciting era of digital transformation. The social platforms serve as a testament to the untapped power of virtual networks, opening doorways to enriching conversations and cutting-edge knowledge sharing in the realm of agriculture.

In essence, social media provides a platform for effective advocacy, dedicated education channels, and most importantly, an engaged community. It illuminates the path to a future where virtual plowing of information will go hand in hand with the physical tilling of the soil, where every farmer is a netizen, and every netizen understands the significance of farming. A world where agriculture doesn't just survive, but thrives, one click at a time.

Chapter 9. Leveraging Social Media for Sustainable Farming Innovations

In an age propelled by digital advances, the stirrings of a revolution have touched the soil-rugged hands shaping our earth. Poetic metaphors aside, the facelift in farming practices stems from an unlikely pairing: social media and sustainable agriculture. This chapter aims to illuminate the ways in which this partnership is not only changing the face of agriculture but also bridging the gap between consumers and the authentic agrarian practices that sustain them.

9.1. From Broadcasting to Narrowcasting

Traditionally, farming information was often disseminated through mass media in a one-directional manner, largely secluded from the consumer. This phenomenon, termed 'broadcasting', allowed little to no room for interaction. Today, however, communication has evolved. The advent of social media has given rise to a new concept — 'narrowcasting'. A term coined to denote specialized sharing of information to a targeted, interested group, narrowing the knowledge dissemination process to create symbiotic learning environments. From farmers using YouTube channels to share crop rotation strategies, to Instagram handles focusing on permaculture principles, social media uniquely tailors to niche segments with specific interests.

9.2. Sustainable Farming Practices via Social Media

Advocates of sustainable farming began using social platforms to share strange-sounding agricultural methodologies like cover cropping, organic farming, CSA shares, permaculture planning, and regenerative agriculture. Communicating these methods and their benefits isn't only for the benefit of other farmers; it provides consumers with transparency, offering them an understanding of what truly goes into their food production.

As potential consumers follow these farm journeys online, they enter into digital relationships, which in turn fuels sustainability. While the customer gets to know the people who produce their food and the practices they use, farmers can tap into broader markets, and advocate for policies that favor sustainable farming. This interaction not only promotes innovation but also transcends the limitation of physical geography, thereby fostering a global community for sustainable farming.

9.3. Case Study: #Farm365 and Real-Time Education

A case that perfectly illustrates social media's impact on sustainable agriculture practices is the #Farm365 hashtag. Initiated by a Canadian dairy farmer, he resolved to post a picture each day for a full year to provide the public with an unfiltered look at the realities of farming. The intention was initially only to document the daily life, work, and care given to the animals. However, it rapidly mushroomed into a global movement. Other farmers joined in, and the hashtag became a platform to educate the public on farming best practices and the importance of sustainable and ethical farming.

9.4. The Rise of Agritech Platforms

Apart from the popular social media platforms, a unique trend is the rise in agritech platforms such as AgFuse and WeFarm, which focus primarily on connecting farmers and sharing agricultural knowledge. Access to new research, discussions on innovative farming practices, climate-adaptation actions, and tips on integrating technology are shared in these forums. Combining the power of social networks with an integrated perspective on sustainability, these platforms are evolving into vital tools for the modern farmer.

9.5. Challenges and Potential Solutions

Despite the unifying power of social media, challenges persist. For instance, navigating the surplus information can be daunting. Similarly, digital illiteracy can pose hindrances, particularly for older-generation farmers. Also, unreliable or biased sources can often misguide readers and disseminate misinformation. To tackle these issues, initiatives focusing on digital skills training for farmers are being rolled out, and efforts are being made to promote international standards for information sharing.

9.6. Looking Ahead: A Sustainable, Connected Future

As the world becomes increasingly entangled in the digital web, the agricultural sector is no exception. We stand at a pivotal moment wherein farmers, consumers, and stakeholders can collectively participate in creating a more sustainable future by leveraging social media. From local, real-time problem-solving to global perspectives on sustainability, the digital tools we have at our fingertips are set to revamp the agricultural landscape forever.

Thus, farmers, technologists, educators - gatekeepers of our food web, are urged to continue building this digital bridge. A bridge connecting the gap between the soil and the cloud, where a single hashtag can spark a revolution, one that leads us to a more sustainable and innovative farming future.

Chapter 10. Challenges and Solutions for Digital Engagement in Agriculture

This exciting chapter spotlights unique challenges encountered in the realm of digital engagement in agriculture, alongside real-world solutions that have been instrumental in mitigating these hurdles. It provides readers with a powerful lens to observe the inherent rich complexities, and the disruptive potential harnessed through the symbiotic fusion of technology and farming.

10.1. Hurdling over the Digital Divide

One of the most prominent challenges faced within this context is the digital divide. The digital divide refers to the gap that exists between individuals, businesses, and geographic areas at different socio-economic levels with regard to both their access to information and communication technology, and their use of it. This effect can be especially pronounced in rural areas where access to reliable, high-speed internet can be scarce. It's no secret that robust internet connectivity forms the very lifeblood of effective social media engagement.

However, triumphs are being scored against this challenge largely through governmental and non-governmental efforts to ramp up rural broadband connectivity. Recently, there has been a surge in initiatives aimed at bridging this digital divide. Various national broadband plans aim to provide pervasive coverage and affordable prices even in remote farming regions. In this vein, the potential for new technologies such as 5G or satellite internet services is also being explored. While it doesn't erase the issue entirely, these concerted efforts have begun to level the digital playing field.

10.2. Battling Digital Illiteracy

Often, farmers and farming communities may not possess the necessary digital literacy skills to harness the power of social media. Unaccustomed to digital interfaces, the learning curve can be quite steep. This digital literacy barrier can inadvertently alienate them, curbing their enthusiasm and leaving room for substantial untapped potential.

Fighting back against this challenge, organizations are organizing workshops and training programs to increase the digital literacy rate in farming communities. They prioritize a hands-on, practical approach, starting from the very basics and gradually navigating towards more complex waters of digital interaction. For instance, farmers are introduced to user-friendly smartphones, educated about basic functions, and eventually led to exploiting the agrarian potential of social media applications. The transformative results of such training sessions have served as a testament to their effectiveness.

10.3. Navigating the Noise of Misinformation

In the current age of information abundance, the distinction between credible and counterfeit information has blurred. The vast swathes of available agricultural information online, despite their accessibility, can often be misleading. Misinformation and false claims can seep into the community, clouding judgment and leading farmers astray.

To combat this, the propagation of validated information through trusted channels and influencers has gained momentum. Online verification tools and fact-checking websites are on the rise, and initiatives encouraging users to critically evaluate information before acting upon it have been widely promoted. It's crucial for the farming community to be equipped to discern between authentic information and deceptive misinformation.

10.4. Mitigating Privacy and Data Security Concerns

The invasion of privacy and threats to data security have escalated with increasing digital engagement. The leakage of sensitive data can compromise the economic security of farming businesses, creating an atmosphere of trepidation and mistrust.

Presently, technologies such as encryption and two-factor authentication have been immensely beneficial in shielding agricultural data. Moreover, by educating farmers about maintaining strong, unique passwords and the importance of frequently updated security software, their susceptibility to these threats can be significantly reduced. Awareness about potential phishing scams and guidance on secure internet behavior play crucial roles in warding off cyber threats.

10.5. Overcoming the Resistance to Change

Culture, as we know, is not static. It evolves over time, and these changes can sometimes be met with significant resistance. The infusion of modern social media techniques into traditional farming can be similarly viewed with apprehension.

Subduing this resistance, many organizations are combining technology with localized context and customs. They are illustrating that these new methods are an extension, an enhancement, rather than a replacement of traditional practices. They portray technology as an ally that enables farmers to optimize their work more efficiently and effectively. Curating experiences that are culturally relevant and relatable has proven to be a winning strategy in countering resistance to change.

In conclusion, by acknowledging the existence of these obstacles and actively seeking out solutions, we pave the way for the deep-seated integration of social media into the agriculture industry. While the negative impacts of these challenges are not to be ignored, the plethora of solutions available to address them reflects that they can be surmounted. Hence, a successful interplay between the agricultural ecosystem and social media would not only benefit the farmers but would also create ripple effects that could stand to benefit society as a whole in the long run. As we stand on the precipice of a digital revolution in agriculture, it behooves us to embrace the bountiful potential it affords us.

Chapter 11. The Future of Agriculture: Social Media and Beyond

The dawn of social media has proven its transformative potential across various facets of life and sectors of the economy. Its infiltration into the agricultural sector, albeit unexpected, demonstrates a new wave of revolutionary trends – a significant shift from conventionally established farming practices to more technologically-advanced and innovative systems. As we peer curiously into this era where digital tides challenge the historical narrative of agriculture, vehement debates arise that deliberate on the scope, impacts, and future of social media's leverage in agriculture.

11.1. A Futuristic Perspective: Social Media - The New Brains of Agriculture

The agricultural sector stands on the brink of a digital renaissance, with social media acting as a central cog, driving this industrious evolution. The future of agriculture might not constitute of just soil, crop, and water; algorithms, hashtags, and gigabytes are set to be integral components, redefining the entire agro-dynamic. The digital makeover of farming is not a mere prediction, but an active metamorphosis signaling paradigm-changing trends.

Farmers of tomorrow might not solely lean onto their ploughs, but also their smartphones brimming with trending farming techniques, crop market prices, and agricultural community discussions. They might trade the humdrum of physical markets for virtual marketplaces where they can sell their produce backed by direct consumer feedback and popularity scores.

Social media's power extends beyond mere communication, information sharing, and virtual community building. It acts as a resourceful farming tool, an extension of the farmer's hand, reaching out across geographical boundaries to gather real-time data, resources, advice, and market stats. Social media will serve as a bridge connecting the farming community with the world at large, empowering farmers with a voice louder than ever.

11.2. The Integration of AI and Social Media in Agriculture

Beyond the practical realms of social interactions, social media's potential lies in its compatibility with artificial intelligence (AI). The fusion of these technologies will present new horizons where AI-integrated social media applications allow farmers to forecast market trends, predict crop outcomes, and perform analytics-driven farming practices.

The growth of AI-augmented reality solutions, powered through common social media platforms, will enable farmers to virtually visit farms across the globe, allowing an exchange of knowledge, skill, and expertise. Such advanced methods could potentially lead to global co-operative farming, fostering solidarity within the agricultural community.

AI's compatibility with social media data boosts precision and smart agriculture. Alert systems to detect anomalies in crops based on global farming data, prediction models for weather or market trends based on billions of social posts, and digital twins for farming strategies will be feasible as social media drives forth an era of data-enriched farming.

11.3. Crafting Policy Frameworks for Social Media Usage in Agriculture

Looking at the potential implications of such a drastic digital shift, the need for robust policy frameworks becomes imminent. Regulation of social media in agriculture, data protection rules, guidelines to counter misinformation, and policies regarding AI ethics are some of the key areas that need dire attention. While technological advancements promise a brighter future, they also bring along potential pitfalls that demand rigorous validation, verification, and regulatory mechanisms in place.

11.4. Collaborations and Partnerships: A Digital Agricultural Network

The fusion of corporate entities, technology start-ups, farming communities, and government bodies will become critical in facilitating and sustaining the digital transformation of agriculture. A collective push towards creating awareness, promoting digital literacy amongst farmers, and setting up digital platforms to foster the integration of social media with agriculture seems likely. These collaborations will play an instrumental role in building digital agricultural networks strengthening the sector.

In conclusion, the future of agriculture holds immense possibilities with the infusion of social media. As we gradually tread towards this digital transformation, it becomes essential to embrace this shift thoughtfully, mindfully maneuvering through the challenges to make best use of the promising opportunities lying ahead. The future doesn't just belong to those who sow seeds in the soil, but also to those who sow hashtags in the digital sphere and give birth to a new era in agriculture.